How To Buy Land When You're Broke & Build A Family Farm

Ishayar

Disclaimer:
This book provides information based on the author's research, personal experience, and best practices in land and home ownership, financing, and farming. This information is intended for educational purposes only and should not be considered legal, financial, or professional advice. Readers are encouraged to consult qualified professionals to address individual circumstances. Neither the author nor the publisher shall be held liable for damages or losses resulting from the application or misinterpretation of the information provided.

Table of Contents

Chapter 1: Find Your Why

As you embark on the journey of building your farm or homestead, one of the most important questions you need to ask yourself is: *Why am I doing this?* Your motivation is key to your long-term success, so it's crucial to get clarity on your purpose early on. Are you building your farm for investment purposes? Are you seeking validation from others on social media because the concept of homesteading has become a popular trend? Or are you genuinely motivated by a desire to create something lasting and beneficial for your family, children, and community?

From my experience, the deepest and most lasting sense of motivation comes from having a purpose that goes beyond yourself. It might be rooted in securing a sustainable future for your loved ones, contributing to your community, or addressing larger societal needs. For example, my journey began out of a desire for shelter and security, not just for me, but for my family and community. I saw how housing was becoming increasingly unaffordable, and I wanted to create a refuge—a self-sustaining space where we could have access to clean water, food, and energy in case of disaster. This bigger vision gave me the strength to push through the difficult times and the persistence to follow through. If your "why" is rooted in something larger than yourself, something that benefits others and has long-term value, you're far more likely to stay committed, even when challenges arise.

However, if your motivation is rooted in external validation or fleeting trends, there's a chance you might not finish the journey. Social media likes or short-term success might not be enough to keep you going when the work gets tough. So, I encourage you to reflect deeply on your *why*. If you're driven by a genuine, meaningful purpose, you're ready to move forward. If not, take some time to rethink your approach.

Chapter 2: Buying Land
Home First, Land Second

When making the transition from city life to rural living, I strongly suggest focusing on securing a home before focusing on land. Here's why: there are far more programs and assistance available to help you purchase a home than there are for buying vacant land. Taking advantage of these resources can ease the financial burden significantly.

Let's think about this practically. If you purchase a piece of land with no home on it, you'll still need to build the infrastructure—water, electricity, sewage, and housing—before you can settle there. This can be expensive and time-consuming. On the other hand, by purchasing a home first, especially in a rural area, you can benefit from grants and loans like rural development loans and first-time homebuyer programs. Even if you've owned a home in the past, you may still qualify for many of these programs if you haven't purchased a new home in the last three years.

A home in a rural area often comes with land, and sometimes with added bonuses like existing infrastructure. You might find a property that already has a barn, chicken coops, or dog kennels, giving you a head start on your homesteading plans. From there, you can focus on expanding and improving the land rather than starting completely from scratch.

That said, there are times when purchasing land first makes sense—perhaps you've found the perfect piece of property at a great price, or a family member has given you land. In those cases, building from the ground up is still a viable option, and we’ll discuss how to do that in later chapters. But for most people starting this journey, buying a home with land already attached is often the smartest route. It provides a stable base to work from and allows you to gradually build the infrastructure you need.

By focusing on the home first and land second, you set yourself up for success, ensuring you have a strong foundation—both literally and financially—for your future farm or homestead.

Financial Assistance

If you're dreaming of owning land but feeling held back by finances, let me share some encouragement from my own journey. Buying a home first can be a game changer. It allows you to settle into a comfortable space without the pressure of building or waiting for a new home. So, when you're looking at land, I highly recommend focusing on properties that already have a home on them. This way, you can enjoy the benefits of rural living without the added stress of starting from scratch.

Now, I know the idea of purchasing land can seem daunting, especially when finances come into play. But here's where the USDA Rural Development Loan comes in, and it's a powerful tool for making your dreams a reality. This program is specifically designed to help folks like us, who aspire to own a home in those beautiful rural areas but may not have that financial cushion to fall back on.

One option to consider is a USDA Rural Development loan. This mortgage program is designed by the United States Department of Agriculture to encourage homeownership in rural areas. It's aimed at moderate- to low-income families, which means if you meet the income requirements, you could qualify for a loan to buy land in eligible areas. You can often get these loans with little to no down payment, and the repayment terms can stretch out to 33 years, making monthly payments more manageable. Even if your credit isn't perfect, there's hope! While some lenders look for a minimum score of 620, the USDA itself doesn't set a hard limit. If your score is lower, your loan just goes through

a manual process, which considers your overall financial situation.
Another fantastic resource is the NACA Program, offered by the Neighborhood Assistance Corporation of America. This program is especially geared towards helping those with low to moderate incomes, or even those with credit challenges. NACA stands out because it doesn't require a down payment, closing costs, or private mortgage insurance. Plus, you'll get some great support throughout the application process. Start by attending a workshop to learn all the ins and outs, then work with a counselor who will help you navigate everything from your application to securing the best possible deal.
You should also look into HUD assistance programs, particularly if you're already receiving rental

assistance. HUD can help low-income families with a portion of mortgage payments. Your local Public Housing Authority can guide you through the options available in your area, and you may even have access to counseling services to assist you on your path to homeownership.

Don't overlook grants for land purchases, either. While they can be a bit more competitive, they don't need to be repaid, making them a sweet deal if you can find one that fits your needs. Grants are often tied to specific uses for the land, like conservation or community development, so do your homework and see what's out there.

Lastly, think about owner financing. This can be a game changer for those who might struggle with traditional bank loans. It offers flexibility in terms of business and potentially lower interest rates. Plus, the process is often simpler and quicker than going through conventional mortgage channels. So, take heart! There are pathways available to make your land ownership dreams a reality. Explore your options, ask questions, and remember that with determination and the right resources, you can achieve that dream of owning your piece of land. Keep pushing forward—you've got this!

Where & What to Look For?

Here are some sites you can check in your specific State featuring land for sale on the market:

LAND AND FARM
LAND WATCH
LAND SEARCH
CRAIGSLIST
LAND LEADER
ZILLOW
REALTOR.COM
TRULIA
LANDS OF AMERICA
CCL
LAND FLIP
DISCOUNTLOTS
BILLY LAND

When you're thinking about buying land, whether it's for living, farming, or just for fun, there are some key things you need to check out to make sure it fits your plans. From my own experience, location is the first thing to think about. You want to make sure the land is easy to get to, whether it's close to main roads or highways. If public transportation is something you'll need, check how accessible it is from the land. Then, there are the basics, like water, electricity, and sewage. You need to find out if these utilities are already available on the land or nearby because adding them can get expensive. I also made sure to check for internet access since staying connected was important for me. Another thing I didn’t know at first was how zoning works—different areas have specific rules about what you can or can’t do with the land. It’s crucial to check this early on, so you don’t run into any roadblocks down the line.

Next, you need to take a good look at the land itself. The physical layout, like whether the land is flat or hilly, can make a big difference depending on what you want to do with it. If you're planning on growing crops or building, knowing the soil type and terrain is important. You also want to pay attention to natural features like rivers, lakes, or wooded areas. While these can add value or beauty to your land, they also come with their own set of challenges, like possible flooding or land management needs. Speaking of water, if you plan on building a house or setting up a septic system, a perc test is essential. This test checks how well the soil drains, and trust me, it's something you don't want to skip. I contacted a local expert to get this done, and it saved me a lot of trouble in the long run. On the legal side of things, checking the title and deed is probably one of the most important steps. When I was buying land, I made sure there were no hidden issues about who owned it or any legal claims on the property. It's also a good idea to get title insurance to protect yourself from any problems that could come up later. You'll also want to check for any easements or rights of way that could affect your use of the land. For instance, if someone else has access to part of your property, like a shared driveway, that could limit what you're able to do. Restrictions like homeowner association rules or deed limitations are also worth looking into, because they can sometimes surprise you with what's allowed and what's not.

One thing I hadn't thought much about at first was the environmental factors. Before buying, I checked whether the land was in a flood zone or if there were wetlands, both of which could limit what you can do with the land. I found the FEMA flood maps super helpful for that. In some cases, the land might have conservation easements, which are restrictions to protect the environment. These are great for preserving nature, but they can also limit how much you can develop the land, so it's important to be aware of them.

Then there's the financial side. Of course, you need to look at the price, but don't forget about the other costs involved, like property taxes and maintenance. If you're taking out a loan, make sure the monthly payments fit within your budget. I also took the time to consider the land's potential to appreciate over time. Looking at nearby development plans can give you an idea of whether the land will increase in value in the future.

If you're planning to build or develop the land, understanding the process for getting permits is key. This can sometimes take longer than expected, so it's good to get a head start on finding out what approvals you'll need. I also looked into the local plans for the area's growth. New developments like schools, businesses, or housing can affect the value of the land in ways you might not expect. Lastly, don't skip the survey. Instead of hiring a surveyor yourself, it's a good idea to request that the seller take care of the survey to mark out the property lines. This way, you're not stuck covering the cost, and if the acreage turns out to be incorrect, the responsibility falls on the seller, not you. It's a smart way to protect yourself from any surprises down the road. You want to be 100% sure about what land you're actually buying. While you're at it, check for any encroachments—like if a neighbor has built something over your boundary line. It's better to sort that out before you buy, trust me on that.

All in all, buying land can be an incredible investment if you do your research. From checking the location and utilities to making sure the legal and environmental factors are clear, taking the time to go through these steps will save you a lot of headaches down the road. Trust me, it's worth every bit of effort.

Land Banks & Tax Delinquent Properties

When it comes to buying land, especially if you're on a budget, *land banks* and *tax delinquent properties* can be real game changers. These are options a lot of people don't know about, but they offer serious opportunities for those of us trying to get ahead without a lot of money in our pockets.

Let's start with *land banks.* A land bank is basically a government program that takes over abandoned or rundown properties that no one wants and makes them available for purchase at a much lower price. These properties might be vacant lots or old buildings, but the key is that they're being sold for way less than market value because the city or county wants to see them put to good use. If you've been struggling to find affordable land, a land bank can offer you a shot at owning a piece of property without having to break the bank. But you've got to be prepared—sometimes these lots need work, and you'll have to have a plan for how you're going to improve or develop the land. It's about seeing the potential and being willing to put in the effort to turn a neglected piece of land into something valuable.

Now, tax-delinquent properties are another hidden gem. When someone doesn't pay their property taxes for a long time, the local government can eventually seize the property and auction it off to recover what's owed. That means you can find land—sometimes with a house on it—at tax auctions way below market value. It's not always as simple as showing up and buying, though. You'll need to do your homework. Make sure the property doesn't have any hidden problems like back taxes or liens. But if you can navigate that process, you can score some serious deals. It's one of the most affordable ways to own land, especially for people who think land ownership is out of reach.

I've seen people turn tax-delinquent properties into family homes, community gardens, or even small farms. It's about being resourceful, staying patient, and understanding that there are opportunities out there if you're willing to dig a little deeper. You might not find your dream property on the first try, but keep at it. You can come across something that, with a little work and vision, can become a steppingstone to the life you've always wanted.

Don't let the fear of not having enough money stop you. There are paths to land ownership that don't require you to be wealthy. Land banks and tax delinquent properties are two of those paths. They're for people like us, people with a dream, some determination, and a willingness to take a chance on land that others have overlooked. You've just got to be willing to take that first step and see the potential where others see problems.

When you're ready to start looking for tax delinquent properties, check out these websites and resources that can help you find listings by city or state:

GovEase

This platform allows you to search for and bid on tax delinquent properties in several states. Many counties across the U.S. use GovEase to conduct their tax lien and tax deed auctions online.

Bid4Assets

Bid4Assets hosts online auctions for

tax lien and tax deed properties. Many local governments use this site to sell properties seized for unpaid taxes. You can search by state or county and participate in auctions directly through the site.

Auction.com

Auction.com specializes in real estate auctions, including tax delinquent properties. You can search for properties by state or zip code and participate in auctions online or in person.

Tax Lien University

This site provides a detailed database of tax delinquent properties available in various states. It's also a great educational resource to help you understand the process of buying tax liens and deeds.

County and City Websites

Many counties and cities post tax delinquent properties directly on their websites, often through the treasurer's or tax assessor's office. Some even host their own online auctions. You can start by searching "[your county/city name] tax delinquent properties" and see if they have an official page with listings or auction information.

Zillow Foreclosures

While not specifically for tax delinquent properties, Zillow does have a foreclosure search feature that can sometimes include tax delinquent listings. It's a user-friendly site where you can set filters by location, price, and property type.

PropertyShark

PropertyShark offers access to foreclosure data, including tax lien and tax delinquent properties in certain areas. It's particularly useful for major cities, providing detailed property reports and auction information.

Just remember, every state and county operates differently, so be sure to check the specific rules in the area you're interested in and always do your homework before making any bids!

Exemptions

An agricultural exemption, or ag use classification, is one of the best tools to help you turn your farming dreams into reality—without breaking the bank. If you're serious about making your land work for you, this is something you don't want to overlook. It's a powerful way to get some major tax breaks, which can be a game-changer when you're working with a tight budget. Here's the good news: It's totally doable, and I'm speaking from experience.

To qualify, you've got to prove that your land is being used primarily for farming—whether that's growing crops, raising livestock, or even managing a forest. It's all about showing that the land is put to good, productive use. Each area has its own rules, so make sure to check what qualifies as "agricultural use" where you are. Sometimes there's a minimum acreage requirement, and in some places, they'll even ask you to show that you're making money off your farm. But don't let that intimidate you—this is part of the process, and it's all about proving your hard work and dedication.

If you're getting into forestry or conservation, you might need to show you've got a plan to manage the land sustainably. It's a little extra paperwork, but trust me, the tax savings are worth every bit of effort you put in. This exemption can slash your property taxes by a lot—because agricultural land gets valued way lower than residential or commercial property. That's how you keep more money in your pocket, and believe me, every bit helps when you're building something from the ground up.

Applying isn't as hard as it sounds. Head over to your local tax assessor's office and submit your proof of agricultural use—whether it's income from your crops, livestock inventories, or a forestry plan. It may seem like a lot at first, but once you've got it, you're set up for long-term savings.

Now, just because you've got the exemption doesn't mean you can sit back and forget about it. You've got to keep things in line and make sure you're still using the land for farming. Local authorities might come out and do inspections just to check that everything's in order. But as long as you stay focused, you'll keep that exemption year after year. Here's the thing, though: While an agricultural exemption can save you a ton of money, it does shape what you can do with the land. You'll need to stick with agriculture to keep those tax benefits, which could mean putting other development plans on hold. But if your goal is to build a sustainable, thriving farm, this is one of the best moves you can make. Stick with it, stay determined, and watch your farm and your future grow!

Considering Distance

When you're choosing land for your homestead, one of the biggest things to think about is how far you're willing to be from essential services. Trust me, it's something you want to get right because it can make or break your experience. You've got to consider how close you want to be to places like Walmart, gas stations, hospitals, and even the local hardware store. Being too far from these things can make daily life a lot harder, especially when you need to grab supplies or handle an emergency. In my experience, being within 25 to 30 miles of major amenities is ideal. It's close enough that you can get to the store, pick up what you need, and still be home in time to work on the farm. But everyone's comfort zone is different—some folks don't mind being 100 miles away from the nearest town, while others prefer staying a bit closer. Think about what works for you, your family, and your lifestyle. It's all about finding that sweet spot where you're far enough to feel the peace and quiet, but not so far that it becomes a hassle.

When I started out, I didn't realize how often we'd need to run out to get building materials, tools, or just groceries. If you're close to these resources, the whole process of setting up your homestead becomes way easier. And don't forget about medical services! If you have kids or health issues, being within a reasonable distance from a hospital is a must.

Moving from the city to the country is an adventure, no doubt about it. But there's an adjustment period. You'll have to get used to the land, learn about the plants and animals around you, and figure out a new way of living. It helps if you're not too far out during this transition. Being close to a city can be like having a safety net while you're getting your feet wet in rural life. Now, there are some major upsides to living farther out—especially when it comes to staying safe from urban chaos. Whether it's a natural disaster, power grid failure, or some kind of civil unrest, being in a rural area can give you a sense of security. But there's a balance to strike. If you're too far away from the city, it could be hard to get help or supplies in an emergency. Sure, people in urban centers might have quicker access to help, but they're also more exposed to the chaos. In a serious disaster, being out in the country can give you an edge, but you don't want to be so isolated that you can't get supplies or medical assistance if you really need it. I learned that being somewhat close to civilization keeps you connected enough to get what you need while still giving you the peace and security that comes with rural living. The key is finding a balance. You want to be close enough to essential services so that daily life isn't a struggle, but far enough away that you can avoid the stress of urban life. It's all about finding a location where you can insulate yourself from the craziness, while still keeping a manageable distance from everything you need. In the end, when you're picking your homestead, really think about how far you're willing to be from conveniences and services. You want to enjoy the benefits of rural life without making it harder on yourself. Once you find that balance, you'll set yourself up for a successful and sustainable homestead.

Buying Land from Locals & Elders

If you have connections in rural areas—whether they are grandparents, former college or high school friends, or acquaintances from online communities—leveraging these relationships can significantly enhance your search for land. Engaging with local residents and establishing connections within the community can often lead to better deals on land than those found through conventional real estate websites like Realtor, Trulia, Zillow, or owner-finance platforms.

Land acquired directly from individuals is frequently more affordable, particularly when dealing with older generations who may own property that has been in their families for generations. Younger family members often do not value this land in the same way and may be more interested in urban lifestyles, which can lead older owners to seek an exit strategy. These landowners may prefer straightforward transactions with honest buyers rather than dealing with realtors or modern technological processes. Such transactions can yield substantial savings, as we have observed properties being acquired for as little as $1,000 per acre through these methods. Additionally, investigating distressed properties—those with rundown buildings or properties where taxes have not been paid—can uncover opportunities to purchase land at a significant discount. By contacting county offices to identify owners of such properties and offering to purchase, you can often acquire land at a fraction of its value, benefiting both you and the seller by preventing foreclosure and providing them with immediate cash.

Adopt A Lot

The *Adopt-a-Lot* program is something I’ve come across when doing my research. It’s a city program that lets you take over a vacant lot for a little while, for free or at a low cost. You don’t own the land, but you get to use it for things like gardening or building a community space. It's a chance to get your hands in the dirt and make something out of nothing, even if the land isn’t yours permanently.

Now, let me be real—this is not a long-term fix. You don’t own the lot, and the city can take it back whenever they need to. So, if you’re dreaming about something you can pass down to your kids or a piece of land that’s truly yours, this isn't it. But for those of us who need a starting point, when buying land is out of reach, it’s a step in the right direction. You get to learn, grow, and work the land while you're figuring out your next move.

I'll be honest, there are limitations. You can't just go and build a house or put up permanent structures. The rules are pretty strict about what you can do, and you have to stay within those lines. But don't let that discourage you. This is an opportunity. It's a way to start something, to be active, to turn an empty lot into something meaningful for yourself and your community.

The *Adopt-a-Lot* program is a steppingstone, not the final destination. It's for those of us who are serious about building a future but need a temporary solution while we save for that piece of land with a home on it. When you can't afford to buy right now, this program gives you a chance to start where you are, with what you have. Use it wisely, but always keep your eyes on the bigger prize—owning your land, owning your future.

Zoning

When selecting land for your homestead or development project, it's crucial to understand the zoning regulations and the significance of unrestricted land. Unrestricted property offers the greatest flexibility for your plans, allowing you to fully utilize the land without the constraints imposed by restrictive zoning laws. This type of property is particularly valuable if you intend to develop raw land that has not been previously utilized, often characterized by dense vegetation and natural terrain.

However, it's important to recognize that even in areas labeled as unrestricted, local counties may still impose specific rules and regulations. A common requirement across many jurisdictions is the percolation test, which assesses the land's ability to absorb moisture.

This test is essential for determining whether the land can effectively manage wastewater, preventing it from pooling on the surface or contaminating nearby water sources.

To perform a basic percolation test, you can pour water onto the land and observe its absorption rate. If the water remains on the surface after 15 minutes, it indicates poor percolation, which could lead to problems with passing official percolation tests. Counties generally require that wastewater be absorbed into the ground rather than sitting on top, in order to protect environmental and public health. Before initiating any development or placing structures on the land, ensure that the property passes the percolation test. Failing to do so could result in costly consequences, including fines and mandates to relocate or cease construction. There are instances where communities have faced significant challenges and even shutdowns due to non-compliance with local regulations. To avoid these issues, thoroughly research and verify zoning requirements and percolation regulations for your chosen land. Even if the property is categorized as unrestricted, it's essential to confirm that it meets all necessary criteria to avoid future complications and ensure the success of your project.

Natural Water Source

When selecting land for your homestead, it is essential to ensure that it includes a reliable source of water. This source can significantly impact the sustainability and safety of your property, providing crucial benefits for your family's needs. Even if the property has access to city water nearby, having a natural water source—such as a spring, stream, pond, or lake—on the property can be a lifesaver in emergency situations.
A natural water source provides not only a dependable supply for drinking, irrigation, and livestock but also a measure of security in case of disruptions to city water services. If possible, choose a property where the water source is situated at a lower elevation than the highest point on the land. This consideration helps mitigate potential flooding

issues, as water will naturally flow downhill, reducing the risk of water accumulation around your home. Historically, the importance of clean, accessible water has been underscored by past events such as the bubonic plague, which claimed millions of lives largely due to poor sanitation and water accessibility. Ensuring that your property has a flowing body of water can therefore be a critical investment in your family's well-being and resilience.

In summary, securing a property with a reliable and accessible water source will not only support your daily needs but also enhance your property's long-term value and safety.

Mineral Rights

When you're thinking about buying land, one of the first things you'll want to check is who owns the mineral rights. It's not something that comes to mind right away, but trust me, it's crucial. In many states, owning the land doesn't always mean you own what's under it. You could buy a piece of property, only to find out later that someone else has the right to drill for oil, gas, or minerals right on your land—without your permission. Crazy, right? That's why it's important to dig into the details.

When you buy land, you usually get the surface rights, which means you own everything you can see: the soil, trees, water, and all the land you walk on. But that doesn't automatically include what's beneath the surface—those mineral rights. Whoever holds those mineral rights has the power to come in and start digging up resources like oil or gas, and they don't even need your say-so to do it.

Now, here's the thing. If someone else owns those mineral rights, they could end up drilling on your property. Imagine buying what you think is your dream piece of land, and then, years later, an oil company rolls in and starts setting up drilling operations. You didn't plan for that, and it can be a real headache. The worst part is, they have every legal right to do it. That's why it's so important to find out upfront whether those rights come with the property or not.

If the mineral rights aren't included with the land, make sure you're getting a good deal. Honestly, it's a huge factor that affects the value of the property. You might want to negotiate for a lower price because, let's face it, not having control over what's beneath the land isn't ideal. It's always better to have the full picture and make sure the price reflects what you're actually getting. Here's another thing to keep in mind: property isn't just about the land you see in front of you. There are all sorts of other rights and interests that come into play. You've got surface rights, but then there are air rights, water rights, timber rights, and even easements that allow others to use parts of your land. These can all affect what you can and can't do with your property, so it's worth understanding them before you sign on the dotted line. For example, if you've got air rights, you could build upward or maybe even sell those rights to a nearby property. Water rights are especially important if your land has access to a stream or river—you want to know if you can use that water for your homestead or farm. Timber rights let you harvest trees and sell the wood, but sometimes, those rights are sold off separately. And then, there are easements—other people may have the right to use a part of your land for things like utility lines or roads. You don't want to be surprised later when someone comes walking across your yard because they've got a legal right to do so.

Each one of these rights can affect the way you use the property and its overall value. That's why it's important to know what you're getting into. Zoning laws, conservation easements, or restrictions can also limit what you can build or how you can use the land. The more you know upfront, the fewer surprises you'll face down the road.

At the end of the day, understanding these rights isn't just about protecting your investment—

it's about making sure the land works for you and your future plans. Buying land is a big step, but if you're smart about it and do your homework, you can avoid a lot of potential headaches. When you know exactly what you're getting into, you can set yourself up for success and build the dream life you've been working toward.

Land Accessibility During Development

If you're thinking about developing raw land, one thing I've learned from experience is that a gradual transition can make the whole process a lot smoother. When we first bought our land, instead of moving onto it right away, we rented an apartment in the city nearby. This gave us the flexibility to commute back and forth, working on the land little by little until we were ready to make the full move. This strategy worked for us in several ways. First off, it's cost-effective. In rural areas, apartments tend to be much cheaper than what you'd find in the city. So, while we were paying less for rent, we were able to put more of our money into developing the land—whether that meant making payments or financing the property. Every dollar saved on rent was another dollar we could put toward turning that raw land into our dream homestead.

Another huge benefit is that it allowed us to tackle the development work at our own pace. Instead of trying to do everything all at once, we'd head out to the land on weekends or after work, doing things like clearing trees, building a dirt pad, or laying down a road. Little by little, we made progress. And when it was finally time to move onto the land, a lot of the heavy lifting was already done.

Now, if you're not buying land with a house on it right away, that's okay too. There are plenty of temporary housing solutions that can work while you get things ready. For example, we considered parking an RV or even setting up a single-wide trailer. You can often find used ones for just a few thousand dollars or less. Sure, they might need a little repair, but they can offer a roof over your head while you keep working on your land.

Let me tell you, jumping straight from city living to undeveloped land with no infrastructure is not easy. That's why this transitional strategy is so helpful—it keeps things manageable. You get the best of both worlds: the comfort of a place to live while making steady progress on your future homestead.

So, if you're thinking about making a move like this, plan it out carefully. Take your time. Use the resources you have wisely, and trust that each step forward gets you closer to living the life you've always wanted.

Chapter 3: Financing Options & Programs

Owner Financing

Let me break it down for you from my own experience: owner financing for land is a powerful option when you're looking to buy. Here's how it works: instead of going to a bank and dealing with all the hassle of a traditional mortgage, the seller of the land—let's call them the owner—steps up and becomes your lender. It's a direct deal between you and them, which can really simplify things. When you're negotiating the terms of owner financing, it's all about finding common ground with the seller. You agree on a purchase price for the land, and usually, the down payment you'll need to put down is less than what a bank would require. That means you might be able to get into that piece of land without breaking the bank right off the bat. You'll also talk about the interest rate on the remaining balance, which can be more favorable than traditional loans. Then, you'll work out a repayment schedule, deciding how long you'll take to pay it off and how often those payments will be made. Plus, the owner will likely keep some kind of security interest in the property until you've fully paid it off, which is standard practice. Now, let's talk about the benefits. One of the biggest perks of owner financing is accessibility. If your credit history isn't perfect or your income isn't where you'd like it to be, this option can open doors for you. You might find yourself able to negotiate terms that work better for you—think lower interest rates or a repayment schedule that fits your budget.

Another thing to consider is the simplicity of the process. You can often avoid a lot of the closing costs and red tape that come with conventional loans, leading to a quicker closing process. In short, if you're looking to buy land, owner financing can be a game changer, putting you on the path to ownership without the usual barriers. Keep your head up and know that with the right approach, that dream of owning your own land is well within reach! Here are several websites that offer owner-financed land-purchasing options:

1. LandWatch
landwatch.com
A comprehensive platform for buying land, with filters to specifically search for owner-financed properties.
2. LandFlip
landflip.com

This site provides a wide variety of land listings, including owner-financed options, with advanced search filters.

3. LandCentral
landcentral.com
Specializes in offering owner-financed land with easy financing terms and no credit checks.

4. Owner Financed Land
ownerfinancedland.com
Focuses exclusively on owner-financed properties, offering flexible terms and detailed property information.

5. Rural Vacant Land
ruralvacantland.com
This site specializes in rural land, many with owner financing, and offers low-cost parcels with easy terms.

6. Classic Country Land
classiccountryland.com
Offers rural and undeveloped land

for sale, including many properties with owner financing.

7. BillyLand

billyland.com

A land auction site that often features owner-financed properties at affordable prices.

8. Acreage for Less

acreageforless.com

Specializes in selling land with easy owner-financing terms and no credit checks.

9. Land And Farm

landandfarm.com

A large listing platform for land, with a filter to search specifically for owner-financed properties.

10. LandHub

landhub.com

Offers a wide range of land listings, including a dedicated section for owner-financed properties.

11. Cheap Lands

cheaplands.com

Features low-cost land across the

U.S., with many owner-financed options.

12. Southeastern Land Group
selandgroup.com
Specializes in rural land in the southeastern U.S., with owner-financed listings available.

13. American Forest Lands
americanforestlands.com
Offers owner-financed rural and recreational land, often with no credit checks.

14. Compass Land USA
compasslandusa.com
Provides land for sale with owner financing, focusing on rural and undeveloped properties.

15. EarthWorks Land
earthworksland.com
Focuses on owner-financed land deals, providing affordable financing options with low down payments.

16. Government Auction
governmentauction.com
Auctions off land, many with owner-

financing options, offering opportunities to purchase at below-market rates.

17. The Land Spot

thelandspot.com

Offers low-cost vacant land, many with owner-financing options, often without credit checks.

18. Open Lands

openlands.co

Specializes in owner-financed land, providing easy payment options and no credit checks for buyers.

Here are additional websites that offer owner-financed land-purchasing options:

19. Lands of America

landsofamerica.com

A popular platform for rural and agricultural land listings, with filters for owner-financed properties.

20. Easy Land Sell

easylandsell.com

Offers land with owner-financing

options, focusing on quick and easy transactions without credit checks.

21. Rural Land USA
rurallandusa.com
Provides a variety of rural properties, including owner-financed options with easy terms.

22. Westward Land
westwardland.com
Specializes in western U.S. land, offering flexible owner-financing with no credit checks.

23. LandModo
landmodo.com
A marketplace for vacant land, with many listings available for owner financing, often with low down payments.

24. LandHope
landhope.com
Offers a range of properties with owner financing, focusing on low-cost land for homesteads and investment.

25. Freedom Land Group
freedomlandgroup.com
Specializes in affordable land for sale with owner financing, offering flexible payment plans.

26. Generation Family Properties
generationfamilyproperties.com
Offers rural and recreational land with owner-financing options, often with no background or credit checks.

27. Classic Land Deals
classiclanddeals.com
Provides low-cost land with owner-financing options, focusing on rural properties across the U.S.

28. GreenLeaf Land
greenleafland.com
Offers affordable land with owner-financing options, typically aimed at recreational and rural buyers. These platforms provide diverse owner-financed land options, making it easier for buyers to find the right property with favorable payment terms.

Chapter 4: Structuring The Land

When you're planning your layout, it's all about thinking smart. You want to position your home, barns, and gardens in ways that work with your daily routine. Pay attention to the sun and wind—those natural elements can make a huge difference in how well your plants grow and how comfortable your living space is. Grouping similar tasks together is also a game changer. It cuts down on unnecessary trips back and forth, saving you time and energy.

Now, when it comes to livestock and crops, you need to keep them separate. This isn't just about keeping things tidy; it's essential for preventing cross-contamination and using your space wisely. Think about how you'll rotate your pastures to keep your animals healthy and the soil rich. And when you choose your crops, look for ones that work well together. Rotation is vital, so plant things that complement each other seasonally. Sustainability is at the heart of a successful homestead. I've learned that implementing things like rainwater harvesting, solar panels, and even composting toilets can significantly reduce your reliance on outside resources. Plus, planting native plants helps protect the local ecosystem while enhancing biodiversity on your land. As you plan out your farm's development, create a timeline that's realistic. Break it down into manageable phases so you can focus on what's essential first, like securing your water supply and building shelters for your livestock. This phased approach not only helps you manage costs but also prepares you for any unexpected challenges that might come your way. Remember, every step you take is a step toward building the homestead of your dreams. With careful planning and a little patience, you can create a thriving, sustainable space that works for you and your family.

Building Your Farm

When you're starting out, think of your infrastructure as the backbone of everything. Reliable water and electricity are absolute must-haves. You might also want to explore renewable energy sources like solar panels or wind turbines; they can make a big difference in the long run. And don't forget about access roads; they need to be solid enough to handle heavy machinery and vehicles, especially when the weather gets rough.

Now, let's talk about building your home and other structures. This part can be one of the most thrilling experiences of your journey. You'll have to decide if you want to build from scratch, use prefabricated buildings, or renovate what's already there. Whatever route you take, focus on using durable materials that won't break the bank. If you're handy, consider some DIY options to save money. Trust me, it feels great to create something with your own two hands. Fencing is another critical aspect you can't overlook. You need to keep your livestock safe while keeping predators at bay. Choose fencing that fits your animals' needs; sometimes, an electric fence can offer that extra layer of security. And don't forget about securing your home and equipment. Simple things like good locks, cameras, and alarms can make a world of difference. Managing construction costs can be tricky, but there are ways to keep expenses in check. Get creative with DIY projects—things like chicken coops, garden beds, or even simple shelters can save you a ton of money. It's perfectly fine to hire professionals for the more complex stuff, but don't shy away from rolling up your sleeves and tackling smaller projects yourself.

Remember, every step you take in building your farm is part of a bigger vision. With a little planning, creativity, and hard work, you'll be well on your way to creating a thriving space that you can truly call home. Keep pushing forward; you're building something amazing!

Conservation Programs

If you're like us and looking for ways to make the most out of your land while doing something good for the environment, there are some great programs out there that can help. I've found that one of the best places to start is with the Conservation Reserve Program (CRP). The USDA essentially pays you to take your most sensitive land out of production and plant species that help the environment. It's a nice way to give the land a break and still get something in return.

Another great program we've used is EQIP, or the Environmental Quality Incentives Program. They offer both financial support and expert advice to help you implement practices that improve your soil, water, air, and everything in between. One of the coolest things they offer is the **High-Tunnel Initiative**. This program helps cover the costs of installing high tunnels (or hoop houses), which are essentially like greenhouses. High tunnels can extend your growing season, protect crops from harsh weather, and improve the overall health of your soil. It's a game-changer if you're looking to grow more efficiently while staying environmentally conscious. If you're thinking long-term, the Agricultural Conservation Easement Program (ACEP) might be for you. It provides financial assistance to help preserve your agricultural lands or wetlands. It's like locking in your land for future generations, ensuring it stays protected and productive. There's also the Regional Conservation Partnership Program (RCPP), which is all about teaming up with others—farmers, ranchers, and local organizations—to tackle bigger conservation issues. If you're focused on regional priorities like water quality or soil health, this is where you can collaborate and make a bigger impact. For ongoing conservation, the Conservation Stewardship Program (CSP) rewards you for maintaining and enhancing the conservation practices you've already got in place. It's like being paid for doing what you're already doing, just a little better. I also recommend looking into the Partners for Fish and Wildlife Program. This one helps you restore and protect habitats on your land, especially if you're passionate about wildlife. They offer both technical and financial support, which can really make a difference. Many states also offer their own State Conservation Grants and Easement Programs, so check out what's available locally. These programs often help protect farmland, forests, and open spaces through grants, land acquisitions, or easements. It's a great way to conserve land while keeping it productive. We've worked with local land trusts and nonprofit programs like The Nature Conservancy to conserve land through easements and land donations. These organizations can provide guidance and sometimes financial assistance to help you protect your property.

Water conservation is key, and many states have Watershed Management Programs. These are geared towards improving water quality and reducing runoff, which can really enhance your land's ability to retain water and support crops or livestock.

Depending on where you are, some states offer tax incentives if you keep your land as agricultural, open space, or wildlife habitat. This can mean big savings on property taxes while you do your part for conservation. State Agricultural Preservation Programs like Maryland's provide funds to buy development rights from farmers, ensuring the land stays in agricultural use rather than being sold off for housing developments. It's a powerful way to protect farmland. If you're into sustainability, you can even get involved in Carbon Credit Programs. By adopting practices that sequester carbon, like planting trees or improving soil health, you can sell those credits to companies looking to offset their emissions. It's a nice way to earn some extra income while helping the environment. Lastly, Water Quality Trading programs allow you to earn credits by reducing runoff or making water quality improvements, which can then be sold to companies needing to meet environmental regulations. It's another way to benefit from making positive changes on your land. For those looking for financial support, there are various Sustainable Agriculture Grants and Loans available that help fund eco-friendly farming practices. These programs offer grants or low-interest loans, making it easier to invest in sustainable farming without breaking the bank.

Free Tree Removal

When planning to clear trees from your property, consider utilizing tree removal services as a cost-effective strategy. Tree removal companies may be willing to remove the trees at no charge if you allow them to keep the timber for resale. This arrangement can significantly reduce your costs, as you will not incur any expenses for the removal itself. In our experience, we spent thousands on bulldozers and excavators to clear our land, unaware that such services could be obtained for free through timber companies or tree removal services. To explore this option, search for timber companies or tree removal services on platforms such as Facebook, Craigslist, and Google. It is important to note that these services may not proactively offer free removal. Instead, you should initiate the conversation and propose the arrangement. This proactive approach can help you clear your property efficiently and at no cost.

DIY vs. Contractors

Self-development will be where you gain the most equity in your property. By acting as your own contractor and completing as many projects as possible on your own, you reduce costs, relying on external sources only when necessary or when outsourcing proves more cost-effective. Many of the projects we have undertaken on our land have been self-developed due to the excessive costs associated with hiring contractors. Completing tasks yourself can save you significant amounts of money.

For example, we installed our own well system after receiving a quote of $21,000. By overseeing the project ourselves, we spent under $2,100, resulting in substantial savings. This scenario will be true for most individuals when establishing infrastructure, building fences, and other similar tasks. While not everyone will have the capacity to undertake large-scale projects, many of the tasks, such as building garden beds or greenhouses, are achievable for most people and can save a considerable amount of money. When it comes to clearing your land, don't let a lack of equipment discourage you. You don't need to own the machinery outright. Many contractors rent the equipment they use, and you can do the same for tasks like dozing or excavation. We learned many of these skills by watching YouTube videos and consulting with experienced locals in our community. Much of the equipment is relatively simple to operate, comparable to using a joystick in a video game, especially excavators. With courage and willingness, you can complete a lot of these tasks yourself. However, if you're uncomfortable with certain projects, it's always advisable to seek professional help. For those who can afford to hire contractors, I recommend comparing different professionals. While there are honest contractors, there are also some who may take advantage of you. When hiring, I’ve found it more economical to pay by the job rather than by the hour. When paying by the hour, especially if you're not present to supervise, there's a risk of inefficiency. I’ve experienced instances where machinery was left running without any work being done, leading to unnecessary costs.

On the other hand, when paying for the job, I’ve had contractors complete the work regardless of whether it takes them a day or two weeks. This approach guarantees that you know the cost upfront and receive the work promised. In contrast, hourly payments can lead to inflated costs due to supposed unforeseen circumstances. I've even had legal disputes over such issues, which reinforces the importance of clear agreements. If hiring contractors will cost the same or more than doing the work yourself, it's often better to hire them, especially when time is a critical factor.

That said, there are times when renting machinery and doing the work yourself is more cost-effective. However, consider factors beyond the rental price. For example, transportation of the machinery—do you have the means to transport it, or will you need to pay for delivery and pickup? Some equipment can be transported on a pickup truck, while others may require a semi-truck. Additionally, calculate fuel costs and other associated expenses. In the end, view self-development as an investment. The money you spend on your property is not wasted; it's akin to depositing funds into a high-interest savings account. As you develop the land, you're building equity. If you ever decide to take out a loan against the property or sell it, you'll see a return on your investment. By following the steps we outline, you should only purchase property below current market value, meaning you're starting with some equity. Any improvements you make will only increase that equity further.

DIY Fencing

Many of you purchasing raw or undeveloped land will likely be working within a limited budget, so finding ways to save money is crucial for you and your family. For example, the trees you see behind me are what most loggers would call pulpwood, which they claim has little to no market value. However, I see it differently. While it may not have high value if sold for timber or lumber, it can still be quite useful depending on your needs. If you visit a store like Home Depot or Tractor Supply, you'll find that pine fence posts—measuring six inches in diameter and eight feet long—can cost anywhere from $8.99 to $24.99 each.

But if your land is filled with these trees, you essentially have an abundance of fence posts at your disposal. By cutting them down and treating them, you can save significantly. Even if these posts only last five to seven years, as many online sources suggest based on the soil's moisture content, that's still five years you can use them to secure your animals or protect your crops. And if they eventually rot, you can simply cut down more trees and replace them. The key is to think creatively and not be discouraged by conventional limitations.

Benefits of Solar

While government incentives for new solar systems exist, used solar panels have become incredibly affordable, making them a highly practical option for those on a budget. Batteries have also become much cheaper, making it easier to assemble a cost-effective solar system using used components. For example, we've found 250-watt solar panels for as low as $20 each on platforms like eBay. It's hard to find solar panels more affordable than that. When paired with cost-effective batteries and inverters, such as the EG4 inverters we use, it's possible to build a solar system for a fraction of the typical cost. Even if you're living off the grid in a remote location without access to traditional power sources, you can establish a fully functioning solar system for just a few thousand dollars. This wasn't possible just a few years ago. By combining used solar panels with an EG4 inverter and affordable batteries, it's possible to go completely off-grid for under $10,000. If you have good credit, financing the system is an option, and your monthly payments could easily be lower than what you'd pay for a standard electricity bill. This is definitely worth considering for anyone looking to reduce their reliance on traditional power sources.

Innovative Ways to use Solar Panels

Beyond their traditional use, inexpensive solar panels open opportunities for creative applications. For instance, you could use them to create a roof for livestock shelters or even as part of a fencing system. At $20 per panel, building a privacy fence with solar panels can be cheaper than purchasing standard materials. The key here is to think outside the box. Look at what resources are available to you and how you can repurpose them in innovative ways. Don't rely solely on conventional methods—there's no single "right" way to approach this. The most important thing is to avoid inaction. Analysis paralysis, where overthinking leads to no action, is a common pitfall. Taking some action, even imperfect, is better than doing nothing. I can relate personally—I spent years pondering homesteading before finally taking the plunge. Looking back, I could have started much earlier. The lesson is to stop overcomplicating things and start taking action.

Establishing a Water Filtration System

When we decided to go the well water route, the first step was to get a thorough water test done. This gave us peace of mind, confirming that our water was safe to drink. To stay on top of things, we regularly use test strips to monitor the water quality, because you can never be too careful. One of the best investments we made was installing a reverse osmosis system in our home. This system includes filters that treat the water right as it comes from the well, plus an extra filtration system at our kitchen sink. Now, we only drink water that's been filtered through this system. It's a simple way to add that extra layer of safety. If you're thinking about setting up a filtration system, I can't recommend enough that you look into adding UV light. These ultraviolet lights are excellent for killing off any bacteria that might sneak past other filters. Honestly, the water we produce from our well, when properly filtered, is often cleaner than what you'd get from the city. When choosing a filtration system, think about the quality of your well water and the specific contaminants you want to tackle. Different systems serve different purposes. For example, sediment filters are essential for removing larger particles like sand and dirt from your water. Then you have activated carbon filters, which work wonders for improving taste and removing chemicals like chlorine.

Iron filters can tackle any pesky iron and manganese that might stain your fixtures or affect the flavor of your water. If you're dealing with hard water, water softeners are your friend; they can help eliminate those hard minerals that cause scale buildup in your pipes and appliances.

I've also learned the importance of UV disinfection. It's an effective way to kill bacteria and viruses without using any chemicals, which is a huge plus. And reverse osmosis systems are fantastic for removing a wide range of contaminants, including heavy metals and microorganisms. Whether you choose an under-sink system for drinking water or a whole-house system, you'll be doing your family a big favor.

If you want to go a step further, consider composite filters that combine multiple methods into one system, providing comprehensive filtration. This way, you get all the benefits without the hassle of managing several different systems. Before you decide, it's very important to test your well water to know exactly what you're dealing with. Consider how easy the system is to maintain, how much water you need, and whether the system fits your space and budget. Remember, investing in the right water filtration system is about ensuring you and your loved ones have clean, safe, and great-tasting water every day. So, take that step—you deserve the best!

Chapter 5: Family Compound Establishing Community

When transitioning to a rural area, your most important asset will be the community you build. Finding like-minded individuals who are willing and able to collaborate will be invaluable in achieving your goals. Ideally, it's best to move with a group—whether that's family, friends, or even just a partner—because many of the tasks you'll face will be far more manageable with support. If you're relocating on your own and don't yet have a community, it's essential to connect with the locals right away. In many rural areas, people are eager to help, share information, provide services, and do business. Building relationships with them will be key to your success, so developing strong communication skills is crucial. Overcoming any shyness or hesitation about interacting with others will help you tap into the most valuable resource—people.

As you integrate into the community, consider not only how others can assist you but also how you can be of service to them. This exchange of goods, services, and knowledge strengthens the community and helps everyone thrive. Remember, it takes a village, and being part of a supportive network is essential. Most of us, particularly those motivated by financial considerations in pursuit of freedom, won't be able to navigate this transition alone. Establishing a cooperative community will ease the journey.

Manufactured Homes

The concept of family compounds is becoming increasingly popular, but many people struggle to connect the idealized images they see online with realistic expectations for what they, their families, or communities can achieve. One of the most effective approaches we've discovered for establishing a family compound is utilizing manufactured homes. Here's why. When you own a piece of land and plan to build traditional stick-built homes, you're often required to subdivide the land because most lenders want to retain control over the land until the loan is paid off. This means they typically won’t allow multiple homes on a single piece of property without subdivision. While this is an option, subdividing and building multiple stick-built homes can be prohibitively expensive, especially for those looking to set up a family compound.

Manufactured homes offer a much more affordable solution. The cost per square foot is significantly lower than that of traditional homes, making them a viable option for most families. Moreover, manufactured homes can be financed with chattel loans, which offer a distinct advantage. Chattel loans allow you to finance the home as personal property, separate from the land. This means that if a member of your family or community defaults on their mortgage, only the home is at risk of repossession, not the land itself. This protects one of your most valuable assets—the land—from being lost. In a family compound setting, this is particularly important. If multiple people participate in the purchase of land, you don't want a situation where one person's financial difficulties jeopardize the entire property. With chattel loans, if someone defaults, they lose only their home, not the land. This allows the rest of the community to step in and help them replace their home without risking the land, which is much harder to replace.

Another reason manufactured homes are an excellent option is that they can later be converted into real property, increasing the equity in both the land and the home. This provides flexibility in how you manage and grow your family compound over time.

Additionally, many of the costs associated with setting up a manufactured home, such as preparing the land, installing septic systems, and utilities, can be inflated when managed by the home seller. A smarter approach is to serve as your own contractor, negotiating a budget for utilities and managing the work yourself. This can save tens of thousands of dollars in the long run, as manufactured home companies often charge significantly more than what these services actually cost.

For those interested in purchasing manufactured homes, we provide resources and support tailored to people moving from the city to rural areas. Unlike traditional salespeople, who may only focus on making the sale, we understand the complexities of developing land for a homestead and the adjustments required for such a lifestyle change. Our goal is to offer a one-stop shop, helping you bypass common obstacles and avoid unnecessary costs, ensuring you have the knowledge and tools to build a successful family compound.

In summary, manufactured homes offer a practical, cost-effective way to establish a family compound while protecting your land and reducing financial risk. By serving as your own contractor and leveraging chattel loans, you can set up a sustainable and flexible community environment without the financial burdens typically associated with stick-built homes.

Chapter 6: Obtaining Animals

Acquiring livestock can be expensive, but there are several strategies to make it more affordable. For instance, when looking to buy chickens or ducks, visiting your local Tractor Supply store can be a great option. While they typically sell baby chicks at set prices, keep an eye on the older chicks that have started to feather out. These older chicks are often discounted to as low as $0.50 to $1. Tractor Supply is eager to clear out these birds, so don't be deterred by the listed prices—ask if there are any discounts on chicks that are a bit older.

For larger livestock like goats and sheep, consider attending local livestock auctions. While auctions usually charge fees, showing up early allows you to interact with farmers directly. Many times, you can strike a deal before the animals even go up for bidding. For example, you might be able to negotiate buying multiple goats or sheep at a much lower price, sometimes as low as $35 each—compared to the $200-$250 price tags they might fetch during the auction. Establishing relationships with local farmers is key to making these kinds of deals happen, as they often prefer to sell directly rather than going through the auction process. Another creative way to acquire livestock is through bartering. For instance, if you have valuable items or services, like a breed of high-demand dogs (such as Dogo Argentinos), you can trade them for farm animals. A dog worth $3,500 to $6,000 could potentially be exchanged for several goats, sheep, or even chickens. By thinking outside the box and leveraging what you already have, you can greatly reduce the financial burden of purchasing livestock.

In summary, whether through discount chicks, auction negotiations, or bartering, there are many ways to acquire livestock without breaking the bank. Building relationships with local farmers and thinking creatively will help you find the best deals and grow your farm efficiently. Finding good livestock at a reasonable price can be a bit of a treasure hunt, but it's definitely doable if you know where to look. One of my go-to spots has been local livestock auctions. These places can be goldmines for competitive prices and a variety of animals. You can often find great deals directly from local breeders and farmers. Just keep an eye on local classifieds, agricultural extension offices, or even check out online auction platforms to see when the next one is happening.

Farm supply stores are also worth checking out. Stores like Tractor Supply Co. or local shops often have livestock for sale or can connect you with breeders nearby. Just drop by or give them a call to see what they have available. Another option that has worked for me is online marketplaces. Websites like Craigslist or Facebook Marketplace can be surprisingly useful. You can find all sorts of livestock from private sellers, so make sure to search for local listings or join farming groups in your area to get the inside scoop. Don't overlook livestock breeders and farms, either. When you buy directly from breeders, you often get well-bred animals with good health records. It can be more cost-effective, plus you can trust the quality of what you're getting. You can find breeders through local agricultural societies or online directories, or even ask other farmers for recommendations. Attending agricultural fairs and shows has also been a game-changer for me. These events often feature livestock sales, and they give you the chance to meet breeders in person and inspect the animals before buying. Keep an eye out for local agricultural events in your community. Cooperative extension services can also be a great resource. They often have connections to local livestock producers and can guide you on where to find sales. Just contact your local county extension office to get started.

Don't forget about farm auctions and estate sales. Sometimes, you can snag livestock at lower prices during larger property sales or farm liquidations. Keep an eye on announcements in local newspapers or auction websites for these opportunities. There are also specialized online livestock markets like LivestockMarket.com and Cattle Exchange, where you can search for specific animals and compare prices. It's worth your time to browse these sites for what you need.

Local feed stores can be a hidden gem as well. They often have bulletin boards or connections for local livestock sales. So, pop into your nearest feed store or give them a shout to see if they know of any livestock available. Finally, tap into community networks. Networking with local farmers, ranchers, or homesteading groups on social media can lead you to affordable livestock. Joining local farming or homesteading groups online can be a great way to gather tips and leads.

When you do decide to purchase livestock, make sure to check the health and condition of the animals. Verify where they come from and be aware of any extra costs, like transportation and veterinary care.

Livestock Price Reduction

Timing and market conditions play a significant role in reducing livestock costs. In southern states like Texas, droughts can lead to a drop in livestock prices. During these periods, farmers often sell their animals for a fraction of their usual value, as they struggle with the cost of hay and water, both of which become scarce and expensive. Livestock such as cows, goats, and sheep can be found on platforms like Facebook Marketplace or Craigslist at drastically reduced prices, sometimes as low as $400 to $600 for cattle, which usually sell for much more. This is because many farmers misjudge the amount of land and water they'll need to sustain their animals during dry spells, and they may be forced to sell off livestock to avoid high feeding and watering costs. Timing your purchase during these dry months can save you significant amounts of money. It's crucial to have access to water on your land during such times, whether through a well, pond, or other water sources, to avoid the need to sell your animals in a crisis. This water supply ensures your livestock can thrive, even when others are forced to sell theirs at a loss.

Guardian Animals

Equally important is protecting your livestock from predators, and that's where livestock guardian animals come into play. Without protection, your livestock can quickly become prey to wildlife such as raccoons, opossums, coyotes, and even larger animals like bears and wolves.

The right livestock guardian animal will help prevent such losses. For instance, using dogs like the Dogo Argentino, which, despite their strong prey drive, can be raised with your chickens and other animals from a young age to become trustworthy guardians. If trained correctly, these dogs won't harm your livestock, and their presence alone can deter predators. Once they mature, predators like raccoons and opossums will avoid your farm altogether. Donkeys are another option. They are highly protective and can deter predators, though it's important to raise them alongside your guardian dogs to avoid conflicts. Other effective guardian animals include peacocks, which are known to kill snakes—making them useful if you're trying to protect chicken eggs from snakes. Geese are excellent for warding off hawks and other birds of prey that might target your chickens. Having guardian animals is crucial for preventing the loss of livestock. With the right animals in place, you ensure your livestock continues to be an asset to your farm, providing food, wool, fertilizer, and other resources essential for self-sufficiency. Whether you're protecting chickens, goats, or larger animals, taking these steps will save you money, labor, and heartache in the long run. Choosing a guardian animal is all about their ability to protect your livestock from predators, their temperament, and how well they get along with the animals you already have.

One of the top choices is the Great Pyrenees. These dogs are large, white, and have a gentle nature. They have a strong instinct to guard livestock, which makes them great companions for sheep, goats, and cattle. Another excellent option is the Anatolian Shepherd. These big, strong dogs are incredibly independent and are natural protectors. They do a fantastic job keeping an eye on sheep, goats, and even poultry. Then there's the Kangal. These dogs are not just large and powerful; they have a calm temperament and are courageous. They can stand up to large predators, making them ideal for sheep, goats, and cattle. You might also consider a Maremma Sheepdog. They are medium to large-sized dogs known for their loyalty and protective nature. They build a strong bond with the livestock, making them great for sheep, goats, and poultry as well. Donkeys are another interesting choice. They have a natural instinct to protect their territory and will often get aggressive with predators like coyotes and foxes. Donkeys work particularly well with sheep and goats, but they might not be the best match for larger animals like cattle. Let's not forget about peacocks! These birds are highly alert and can act as an early warning system with their loud calls and keen senses. They're great companions for poultry and other small animals, but they aren't suited for protecting larger livestock.

When picking a livestock guardian animal, there are a few things you should keep in mind. First, look for an animal with a calm and protective nature that meshes well with your livestock. Compatibility is key. Make sure the guardian breed fits your specific livestock and your environment. Training is also crucial. These animals typically need some socialization and training to do their jobs well. Introducing them to your livestock early on can make a big difference. Think about the predators in your area, too. Different guardian animals excel at protecting against certain types of predators, so know what you're up against. Lastly, ensure your guardian animal has enough space to roam and patrol. Some breeds need more room and exercise than others. In the end, choosing the right livestock guardian animal really comes down to your specific needs and circumstances. With the right choice, you’ll have a loyal protector for your livestock!

Chapter 7: Gardening

Gardening is truly the heart of farming, and I can tell you from experience that you don't need a lot of money or fancy gear to get started. Whether you've got a small backyard or you're dreaming of vast fields, there are plenty of ways to grow your garden without breaking the bank. I want to share some simple, cost-effective methods that helped me cultivate a productive garden, and I'm confident you can do it too. First off, you need to assess your space. It doesn't matter if you have a sprawling backyard, a cozy balcony, or just a few windowsills; there's always room to grow something. Take a good look at your available space and the sunlight it gets, and that will help you figure out what type of garden will work best for you. Now, I know it can be tempting to want to plant everything at once, but trust me, starting small is the way to go. By focusing on just a few key plants that are easy to grow and maintain, you'll have a better chance to learn and adjust as you go along. It'll save you time and money, and you won't feel overwhelmed. When it comes to building garden beds, you don't have to spend a fortune on fancy ones. We built our own using reclaimed wood, bricks, or even repurposed containers. This approach not only saves you money but also gives your garden a unique touch that reflects your style.

DIY Gardening Projects

Gardening is an incredible way to get creative while saving some money, and I've found that DIY projects can really boost both your budget and your garden's functionality. For instance, instead of shelling out cash for a compost bin, why not make your own using an old trash can? Just drill some holes in it for aeration, and you've got yourself a composting system that cuts down on waste and enriches your soil—trust me, it's one of the best investments you can make for your garden. Watering can get expensive, but we found a great way to save by collecting rainwater. Just set up a rain barrel under your gutter, and you'll have a free source of water for your plants. You can buy these barrels at hardware stores, or if you're feeling crafty, repurpose some large containers you already have lying around. Keeping track of what you're growing can be a fun project too. You can use popsicle sticks, painted rocks, or even wine corks on skewers to label your plants. It's a creative way to add a personal touch to your garden.

If space is tight, think vertically! Old pallets, shoe organizers, or hanging pots can be transformed into vertical gardens, giving you more growing space without taking up precious ground area. When it comes to pots and raised garden beds, you can get really inventive using materials you already have. For pots, we stacked old tires to create large planters—just paint them for a little flair. Wooden pallets work wonders too; you can turn them into vertical planters or trough-style pots by filling them with soil. Cleaned tin cans make great small pots for herbs or flowers, and if you cut plastic bottles in half, they can serve as nifty little planters for seedlings.

As for raised garden beds, reclaimed wood from old fences or pallets can be put to good use. Just sand and seal it to keep it from rotting. Stacking concrete blocks or bricks is another easy way to create sturdy beds. If you have an old bathtub, you can convert that into a deep raised bed for all kinds of plants. There's really no limit to what you can use; I've even turned old doors into the sides of a raised bed, giving it a unique character. Large plastic storage bins can be cut to create lightweight raised beds, and old furniture like dressers can be repurposed as planters, adding a quirky touch to your garden. By using materials, you already have, not only do you save money, but you also make your gardening space feel uniquely yours. Trust me, there's something incredibly satisfying about creating a garden filled with DIY projects that you crafted yourself!

Gardening Tips

When it comes to making your garden thrive, there are a few things I've learned that really make a difference. First off, knowing your planting zone is key. I remember when we started out, I didn't pay attention to it and wondered why some plants just wouldn't make it. Once I checked the USDA Plant Hardiness Zone Map, everything clicked. It's all about choosing plants that can handle your local climate. You get this right, and you're already ahead of the game. Starting from seeds is another way to go. We used to buy plants, but it adds up fast, and you're limited to whatever the store has. Then we gave seeds a try—way cheaper and way more variety. Plus, some places have seed swaps, like at libraries or community centers, where you can grab seeds for free.

We've gotten some amazing plants that way!
Good soil is the backbone of everything. If your soil isn't right, it doesn't matter what you plant. I made sure to test my soil's pH and then worked on it, adding compost, manure, and organic fertilizers over time. It took a while to get it where I wanted, but once the soil was healthy, the plants just took off.
Mulching is another tip that I swear by. Not only does it keep moisture in the soil, but it also cuts down on weeds—nobody likes weeding! I use straw, leaves, or grass clippings, whatever's around, and it keeps the plants protected and happy.
Now, here's something I didn't know at first—some plants just grow better together. It's called companion planting. For example, basil and tomatoes are like best friends; basil helps keep pests off

the tomatoes. Do a little research, and you'll find some great pairings that make your garden work even better. When it comes to pests, you don't need to jump straight to chemicals. We've had great success using natural methods, like bringing in ladybugs and praying mantises, spraying with neem oil, or putting up barriers to keep the bugs out. It works, and you don't have to worry about spraying harmful stuff all over your plants. Watering can get expensive if you're not careful. What I've found works best is watering either early in the morning or later in the evening when the sun isn't out. This way, you don't lose as much water to evaporation. Also, drip irrigation or soaker hoses are a game changer because they focus on getting water right to the roots where it's needed.

Also, don't forget to harvest often. We used to leave things on the plant too long, thinking they'd get bigger, but regular harvesting actually encourages more growth. Pick those herbs and greens as soon as they're ready, and you'll see the plants keep producing more and more. These little tips have made a huge difference for me, and I know they'll help keep your garden growing strong too.

Conclusion

Celebrating Your Success and Future Planning

Building a farm or homestead is a monumental achievement that deserves recognition. Reflect on your journey, celebrate your successes, and take pride in the community and lifestyle you have created. Continue setting goals and planning for the future, knowing that your efforts are contributing to a sustainable and fulfilling way of life.

Additional Resources for Continuous Learning

Farming and homesteading are lifelong learning experiences. Seek out additional resources, such as books, online courses, and local extension services, to continue expanding your knowledge. Stay curious and open to new ideas, and your farm will thrive for generations to come.

Ready to take the next step?

Your journey doesn't end here—it's just getting started. If you're serious about owning land, building a farm, or simply learning more, join us at www.40acrecomeback.com.

At 40 Acre Comeback, we're a community of dreamers, doers, and future landowners, all working together to make land ownership a reality. Whether you're looking for guidance, a supportive community, or practical tools, we've got you covered.

Join our community: Connect with like-minded individuals, share experiences, and get advice from people who've been in your shoes.

Enroll in our courses: Dive deep into strategies for buying land, building a farm, homeschooling and navigating the land ownership process when funds are tight.

Your future is waiting. Visit us today and let's make your land ownership dreams come true!

www.ingramcontent.com/pod-product-compliance
Ingram Content Group UK Ltd.
Pitfield, Milton Keynes, MK11 3LW, UK
UKHW021657190726
13853UKWH00001B/323